SPEAK THE WORD

Activating the Transforming Power of the Spoken Word for Victorious Living

Dr. Simeon Agbolabori

SPEAK THE WORD!

Copyright © 2022 by Dr. Simeon Agbolabori

ISBN: 978-1-952098-95-6

Printed in the United States of America. All rights reserved solely by the publisher. This book or parts thereof may not be reproduced in any form, stored in a retrieval system, or transmitted in any form by any means - electronic, mechanical, photocopy. Unless otherwise noted, Bible quotations are taken from the Holy Bible, New King James Version. Copyright 1982 by Thomas Nelson, Inc., publishers. Used by permission.

Published By:
Cornerstone Publishing, USA
A division of Cornerstone Creativity Group LLC
Info@thecornerstonepublishers.com
www.thecornerstonepublishers.com

Author's Information
For bulk order of this book or to reach the author, please send email to:
dr.agbolabori@gmail.com or visit
www.bishopsimeonagbolabori.com

FOREWORD

God did not lace up His boots and roll up His sleeves to create the heaven and the earth, He stepped out on absolutely nothing and the power of creation came shooting out of His mouth. God spoke the whole world, the heaven and the earth, the space, the galaxies and everything, both visible and invisible into existence!

God demonstrated to us how efficacious speaking the word is. Also, speaking the word is a potent weapon in the hands of the children of God.

When a man of the word writes about the word, the world better listen. Dr. Simeon Agbolabori, a dear friend of mine, is a man of the word, and in his pursuit of excellence, God has transformed him to an amazing man of God, a compassionate pastor and a lover of people; a God fearing man who will go the whole distance for the kingdom sake.

I am honoured to write the foreword of *Speak the Word*. I read the manuscript of this book with utmost care and attention because the word of God is heavy and if care is not taken, one can easily be deceived and say, "I have read something like it before," meanwhile, God has a completely different revelation for you.

This book offers the blueprint for living and not just existing. When you are not speaking the word to influence your environment both physically and spiritually, you are not living; you are merely existing! What a potent weapon it is, to speak the word of God with accuracy and boldness.

Jesus said in John 16:26, At that day ye shall ask in my name: and I say not unto you, that I will pray the Father for you:

That you shall speak the word by yourself. You shall ask with your own mouth. I will not ask for you. He said.

Dr. Simeon Agbolabori in this book, challenges you to break down the strongholds that keep you locked in self-defeating behaviours and an unfulfilling life by speaking the word into that situation no matter what.

This is the book that will give you that opportunity to make a U-turn and change the course of your life by simply speaking the word. It is a much needed resource for those who are tired of being tired, who have been down for a long time and are losing hope.

Dr Simeon Agbolabori is a quintessential leader. I am captivated by his wealth of experience and his vision of seeing 'ordinary men' becoming the person God made them to be.

In 12 chapters, He gave a life – giving message of faith and action, using his personal life experience and testimonies that are verifiable. He says speaking the word is a demonstration of one's faith. You should speak what you believe with confidence, and at all times. Demonstrate your faith today, because without faith, no man can please God.

I advise that you feast on this book; it will give you nourishment and satisfy you spirit, soul and body.

Apostle Lawrence Achudume
Lead Pastor, Victory Life Bible Church

Dedication

This inspired book is dedicated to God the Father, the Son and the Holy Spirit.

And also to

Dr. Jide & Dr. (Mrs.) Bolaji Olutimehin who stood solidly with me and family since the demise of my wife over 8 years ago.

And to my three wonderful sons: Olayinka Nenaji Agbolabori, Pastor Abimbola Stephen Agbolabori and Toluwanimi Miracle Agbolabori.

To my daughters in-law; Hasifa Kivumbi Agbolabori and Dr. Abimbola Ope Agbolabori and also to my grandson; Jesudarasimi Preston Agbolabori.

And with this book I honor the evergreen memory of my late wife, Rev. (Mrs.) Patricia Olujoke Agbolabori.

Acknowledgments

I acknowledge the contributions and supports of numerous people who have made life and ministry pleasant for me. Their encouragements have been of tremendous motivation too. At the top of the list is Bishop Francis Wale Oke, the President of the Sword of the Spirit Ministries, General Overseer of Christ Life Church, Chancellor of the Precious Cornerstone University and National President of the Pentecostal Fellowship of Nigeria. Others are Bishops Mike and Peace Okonkwo of TREM; Prophet Isa El- Buba, the President of EBOMI; Apostle Lawrence Achudume, the General Overseer of Victory Life Bible Church; Apostle Zilly Aggrey, the General Overseer of Royal House of Grace; Bishop Yomi Isijola, General Overseer of Logos Ministries; Pastor Robert Kayanja of Kampala, Uganda; Reverend Gbenga and Pastor(Dr.) Yinka Kotila; Reverend Sam and Pastor (Mrs.) Moji Alawiye and many more who have been my guests at the Chapel of Restoration, Houston, Texas as well as those who have opened their doors for my gift, calling and grace to work in their congregations.

I would also like to acknowledge all the members of the International Communion of Bishops and Apostles

(ICOBAPS), Greater Houston Ministers Fellowship (GHMF), Simeon Agbolabori Ministries International (SAMI), and the Chapel of Restoration (COR).

I thank in particular some of my friends and colleagues in Houston Texas; Pastor (Dr.) David Babatunde Osho, Pastor Alabi Obiri, Pastor David Arogbonlo, Pastor Ade Okonrende, Bishop Jerome Etinfoh and many others for their brotherly supports over the years.

Finally, salutations to the leadership of the Chapel of Restoration Houston, Texas; from the Resident Pastors; Reverend Eric and Pastor (Mrs.) Uduak Ezeakachi, to Pastor Ashimiyu Adetoyinbo, Pastor Osas Erivo, Pastor Humphrey Ezeakachi and Pastor Grace Olusanya.

What you have all made happen to me it is my prayer that the Lord will make it happen to you in the name of Jesus Christ.

Contents

Introduction...13

1. Knowing the Word....................................17
2. The Creative Ability of the Word.................25
3. Destiny Changing Word..............................37
4. The Impregnated Word...............................49
5. The Commanded Word...............................57
6. The Word of the King................................65
7. The Word of Deliverance............................71
8. Speak to the Wind....................................77
9. Speak to Death..83
10. Speak Healing...91
11. Speak Abundance...................................101
12. Believe and Speak..................................111

Conclusion...115

Introduction

One of the most underutilized kingdom mysteries by believers is the power of the word. The Bible expressly states that the power of life and death is in the tongue (Proverbs 18:21). This infers that by our utterances we have the divine ability to chart the course of our lives and destinies. More so, the scripture gives us several examples of men and women of faith who by their positive persistent faith-driven confessions changed the course of nature and effected desired realities in their lives, the lives of others, communities and nations. Yet, having this much information at our disposal, many believers continue to wallow in pain, rejection, depression, struggles, sicknesses, and various forms of hardships as though our Father has not given us a viable way of escape; the faith-driven declarations of our mouths.

My vision for this book is to reawaken the believer to the power of the word in shaping our world. It is high time we arose to our true calling as kings and priests unto our God (Revelations 1:6) and activate our spiritual authority to make changes in our world. Someone once said that a closed mouth is a closed destiny. How true that is! Many destinies are under a siege because men and women have refused to speak against the forces of limitations hindering them. There is no limit to the beauty that can emerge from our lives when we adopt the spiritual discipline and lifestyle of declaring the word of God consistently, without fear or intimidation.

I am persuaded that there are treasures we are yet to unlock and realms of kingdom manifestations that God would have us live out in our everyday lives if only we can recognize, understand and embrace our duty to declare the word of our God. It is not sufficient to have knowledge of the scriptures and the myriad promises of God loaded within. We must activate its operations in our lives by speaking those words.

Just as the word of God never returns to him without accomplishing the purpose for which it was spoken (Isaiah 55:11), so will your word begin to operate. Remember, the Bible calls us gods, sons of the Most High (Psalms 82:6). God wants us to operate like him in many ways as a testament of our sonship. I am trusting God that as you go through the pages of this book, you will learn, unlearn and relearn this mystery of the word and activate its full function in all areas of your life. I am certain that victory awaits your obedience to the truths and instructions offered by this inspired work. Be blessed as you read in Jesus name. (Amen)

Chapter 1
Knowing the Word

Chapter 1
Knowing the Word

In the Kingdom, when we talk about "The Word", understand that we do not refer to the common utterances of ordinary men or excellent oration born of human wisdom. Rather we speak of the authoritative word of God; the undisputable, incorruptible, and everlasting word. As you journey through this book, you will see how the multifunctional word of God has improved diverse situations.. This same word has calmed storms, healed the sick, delivered the oppressed, given children to the barren, brought abundance into lack, restored sanity to the insane, and raised the dead.

There are several unique attributes of the word of God. One of the fundamental qualities is that unlike the words of men that cannot be relied upon, the word of God is ever dependable. See how the Psalmist put it:

> *"Forever, O Lord, they word is settled in heaven"* Psalm 119:89

This word is not transient, temporary or debatable. It is settled the moment it is uttered. God's word is beyond the wisdom and knowledge of man, it is word spoken in power and authority.

> *"How sweet are thy words unto my taste! Yea sweeter than honey to my mouth"* Psalm 119:10.

The word of God is sweet; it brings delight to the hearer. Unlike mere words that may bring depression or sadness, God's word sweetens and gladdens the heart of the hearer.

> *"Thy word is a lamp unto my feet, and a light unto my path"* Psalm 119:105

This word brings clarity of purpose, dream and vision. It shows direction for life. In other words, the word of God is the compass or navigation device for our ways.

> *"I am afflicted very much: quicken me, O Lord, according unto thy word."* Psalm 119: 107

The word of God is that which gives life to the dying and revitalizes them.

> *"Thou art my hiding place and my shield: I hope in thy word."* Psalm 119: 114

If there is anywhere to put your hope, do so in this unchangeable word of the living God. His word is a place of refuge. As the Psalmist boldly declared that his hope is in the word of God, so should you.

> *"The entrance of thy words giveth light; it giveth understanding unto the simple"* Psalm119:130

The word of God brings intelligence, wisdom and understanding. Wherever the word of God is richly spoken, wisdom, understanding and intelligence abounds.

> *"Thy word is very pure: therefore thy servant loveth it."* Psalm 119: 140

There is purity in the word of God, no corruption can be found in it.

> *"Let my supplication come before thee: deliver me according to thy word"* Psalm 119: 170

If you ever needed deliverance, from any habits, behaviors, spiritual challenges or attacks all you need is the word of God.

There is nothing as terrible as heading in the wrong direction without knowing it. Such venture wastes effort and energy and brings negative influence and results. However, once ones feet are planted directly in the right direction, there is always excitement and joy knowing that success is imminent.

> *"Order my steps in thy word…"* Psalm 119: 133

The word of God was described as the word of truth; we should all pray that such word would not be taken away from our mouth.

> *"And take not the word of truth utterly out of my mouth; for I have hoped in your judgments."* Psalm 119: 43

You can purify your lifestyle through the power in the word. I have said earlier that the word is multi-purpose and it works in every situation, climate, culture and nationality.

> *"Wherewithal shall a young man cleanse his way? By taking heed thereto according to thy word."* Psalm 119:9

Now let's now summarize this by talking about the potency of the word of God.

> *"For the word of God is quick, and powerful, and sharper than any twoedged sword, piercing even to the dividing asunder of soul and spirit, and of the joints and marrow, and is a discerner of thoughts and intents of the heart."* Hebrews 4:12

God's word is the vital tool for casting out evil spirits as demonstrated by Jesus and His disciples in their days. This is contrary to some uninformed methods of exorcism practiced by people who lack adequate knowledge of God's word. Such people subject individuals suspected of demon possession to terrible and inhuman treatment like beating them up, pulling the hairs of women's head, asking them to force passing gas and vomit as an evidence that they are free from demons. The scripture however states that all we need is the word of God. Once you speak the word in faith, no demon can stand against or resist you.

The issue is either you got it or you don't. If you do, you don't have to force it or struggle at it. The word is so powerful that it effortlessly casts out demons. Speaking of Jesus, Matthew 8:16 records "And when the even was come, they brought unto him many that were possessed with devils: and he cast out the spirits with his word, and healed all that were sick."

Evidently, the word of God is alive and living. It is powerful, full of God's authority and it penetrates the body, revealing the activities therein even more than any EKG, MRI or other form of advanced imaging devices. It also can discern the thoughts of man's heart as well as their intentions. Without any doubt, the passages above confirm that the word is beyond ordinary heaping up of sentences. It is the representation of God and His being.

My prayer is that you will take the word of God very seriously and use it to change your life and transform your whole being until your life aligns totally with the word of the living God.

Now, let us go into deeper application of the word as the Bible reveals to us.

Chapter 2
The Creative Ability of the Word

Chapter 2

The Creative Ability of the Word

Creativity speaks of the ability to bring into being or cause to exist. To make this happen, it means whatever is caused to exist or come into being, never existed; such that there was no prototype of it or ever any like it.

That was what God did at creation. He made all things original. They were not copies of any others, and there were none of their kind before then. And amazingly all that were made were not made by any other means but through the power of his spoken word.

All God utilized in bringing the entire universe into existence was his spoken word. This tells you and me that if we would dare act like him we will have a lot of changes surfacing in our lives and around us.

> *"(As it was written, I have made thee a father of many nations) before him whom he believed, even God, who quickeneth the dead, and called those things which be not as though they were." Romans 4:17*

This scripture above was making reference to how God created all that he created. It says he "…called those things which be not as though they were."

Speaking about God, we found out that by his words he addressed things which were not tangible as though they were. Genesis 1 & 2 give the account of God employing the word as the creator of all his six days creation.

Many believers have read and learnt of the creative work of God, how he framed and made all things. It should however, be noted that the creative work was not some sort of manual labor. It was rather a project carried out at the comfort of God's word. God while creating all things did not have to touch anything until he was ready to create man. All he did was speak all things into existence and as soon as he commanded, whatever he called forth came into been. This was done to serve as examples to all of us, that what God did and how he did it is exactly what we should do as well as how we should do them.

Now let us see how God employed His word in the process of creation.

The word says;

> *"In the beginning God created the heaven and the earth"*
> *Genesis 1:1*

This opening tells us that God began the process of creation, the next verse tells us the state of the earth;

> *"And the earth was without form, and void; and darkness was upon the face of the deep. And the Spirit of God moved upon the face of the waters." Genesis 1:2*

The whole earth was without form and it was void, there was no light upon the earth as there was perpetual darkness hovering over the earth.

Beloved, the situation here could be likened to a depressing one as darkness is a symbol of gloom and hopelessness. We all know that the beauty of a thing is revealed by the amount of light on it. That is why you see showrooms with so much light to manifest the beauty of whatever is on display. Darkness can also symbolize the operation of demonic work in one's life or over a nation. It also symbolizes crisis and chaos.

When God saw this, he knew he had to take charge of it and when he was to confront the ugly and depressing situation, he didn't go into any form of physical confrontation. He was not into any acrobatic exuberance like we see now a days but rather he employed the Rhema (the spoken word). He did not conjure light, he commanded light. Believers must be wary of those who claimed to have gone in the name of the Lord but have resorted to employing metaphysics to do the work of the Lord. They are easily recognizable by their fruits very well and not their looks for every tree is known not by its trunk or its leaves but by its fruits. Let no one deceive you by their show of power or ability to do, examine the fruits of their lives.

God called light into existence and because he had faith in what he had spoken, light immediately manifested thereby expelling darkness and bringing beauty into ugliness, joy into sadness and excitement to replace depression.

The earth was said to be without form and it was void. In other words, like lives of many, the earth was shapeless and empty. There was a need for structure and organization. Perhaps, like the earth, your life needs order and organization, I think it would be just fine if you look into how God dealt with the first situation of its kind.

> *"And God said, Let there be light: and there was light"*
> *Genesis 1:3*

Knowing that learning is best done by observation, if you would ever get anything done, if you would ever achieve anything of substance, and if you desire to see a tangible success or progress in your life, you have to observe how God did all he did and imitate him.

Here we see that when God was not happy with darkness controlling the affairs of the day, he didn't resort to whining and complaining about it, which is what some believers do when faced with an unpleasant situation. Instead, God acted decisively by speaking into being that which nullifies and counteracts the activities of darkness. He simply declared "Let there be light" and light came forth in response to his decree.

If you have noticed any activity of devil or evil ones in your life, if you have been sad or depressed about one thing or the other, if you have been in a battle that seems you can't win all alone, or maybe you are faced with challenges that seems insurmountable, my advice to you is to get up and imitate God. You also should take immediate and decisive action just as God did, to call into existence your expectations.

Just like God, you will have whatever you say ONLY if you ask in faith.

The visible was made from the invisible, the tangible from the intangible.

John 1 tells us that without the Word nothing created would have been created.

> *"In the beginning was the Word, and the Word was with God, and the Word was God." John 1: 1*

This verse addressed God as the Word, so now we see how powerful the word can be. If the Word is God, then it has the power of God to effect immediate change. The Word carries the ability and personality of God. No wonder the scripture says "You will decree a thing and it shall be done" if you ask anything without wavering in your mind. . All these and more are possible because the word carries the ability of God.

See how the gospel writer puts God's ability quoting Jesus;

> *"With men this is impossible but with God all things are possible"* Matthew 19:26

So if the Word carries the ability of God, we can then say; "With men this is impossible but with the word all things are possible."

Genesis 1:5 states, *"And God called the light Day, and the darkness Night. And the evening and the morning was the first day."*

Now we see from this passage that God started putting order in place by calling what he had created by their names. He called the light "Day" and darkness "Night".

And it should be observed that the word of God is irrevocable in that whatever He called those periods of time is still what they are now. So you can also call a thing by name and whatever you call them is what they would be only if you have faith in God and your words.

If you called crisis situation in your life peace and you have the faith in God, you will immediately begin to feel peace and serenity around you. If through the eyes of faith you call prosperity out of poverty and you do not have doubt, you will see prosperity coming to you. If you are barren and you begin to lay your hands on your womb or loins and start calling your reproductive organs productive, you will be amazed how God would respond to your faith by putting children in it.

> *"And Jesus answering saith unto them, Have faith in God. For verily I say unto you, That whosoever shall*

say unto this mountain, Be thou removed, and be thou cast into the sea; AND SHALL NOT DOUBT IN HIS HEART, BUT SHALL BELIEVE THAT THOSE THINGS WHICH HE SAITH SHALL COME TO PASS; he shall have whatsoever he saith." Mark 11:22-23 Emphasis is mine.

Breaking this down, here are the simple practical steps to follow:

Firstly, have faith in God. What does that mean? It mean believing that he is the ultimate, he is the almighty, whatever he says is what happens, he is above all and beyond all. You must embrace the understanding that God is absolute in all things, self-ruling, self-governing, and supreme overall. .

Secondly, you must speak to your life and situations around you. Start commanding every mountain of failure, defeat, loss, sickness or whatever constituted itself as a mountain in your life to be removed and "be cast into the sea", never to be seen again.

Thirdly, have no doubt in your heart. Make sure your heart firmly believes what your mouth is saying with the full expectation of having what you are saying. Be convinced that they shall come to pass.

Fourthly, you will see the manifestation of those things that you have asked for.

This sounds like a principle; of course, it is one, and it is the principle that moves heaven to respond to prayer at all time.

God himself followed this principle in that,

1. Even though He is God, He had faith in Himself before ever venturing into speaking.

2. He thought about the situation and what to do with it.

3. He then spoke upon it as He wanted it to be.

4. And with these components in place, He was able to see the manifestation of those things which He has spoken.

> "… even God, who quickeneth the dead, and called those things which be not as though they were" Romans 4:17

You also will have to start creating things in your life, remember that the word said all that God created through His words were very good.

Your lack is no more a lack when you can speak; crisis has no room again if you can create peace. God thought of what to create and he spoke it into being.

Begin to do the same and you will see the dramatic change that would come to your life.

If you continue to follow the recorded account of how God created everything you will realize that it was done through spoken words. You have been equipped to do likewise. You can begin to call forth a pleasant life and a peaceful home, brilliant and well-behaved kids, supportive wife or a loving husband. There are no limits to the new realities you are capable of creating if you will believe and speak.

Chapter 3

Destiny Changing Word

Chapter 3
Destiny Changing Word

"Make a tree good and the fruits thereof shall be good…"
Matthew 12:33

The simple secret to improving the conditions of a fruit is to address the source which is the tree. And by simple utterances of faith, you can change the natural order of things including the elements and all creatures. As exemplified by Jesus, you can in fact turn the destiny of a tree around by just speaking to it.

If you call a good tree bad, with faith in your heart you will immediately see that the fruits of that tree will turn bad. And if you on the order hand speak the word of life to a bad or evil tree, that tree will immediately begin to bring forth good and pleasant fruits. The tree here is a symbol of your life, children, marriage, business, even your health and that of other people.

You can change a destiny with what you say.

Destiny can be reversed by what you say. Many believers do not understand that what the Bible said about life and death is in the power of the tongue (Prov. 18:21) is true, that is why many use their mouth to speak flippantly, uttering careless words. Whereas the tongue, though one of the smallest organ in body, has the greatest power.

The story of the Shunammite woman and Elisha is a very good example of how you can use your words to change destiny. This woman was described as a great woman (2 Kings 4:8). She was great in wealth, possession and influence. She compelled her husband to help make a little chamber for Elisha whom she had perceived to be a servant of God (2 Kings 4:10). The husband subscribed to this suggestion and Elisha enjoyed their hospitality. On one day Elisha wanted to bless this great woman in return for her generosity and hospitality, he then called her to demand of her what her needs were, to this she answered.

"I dwell among mine own people." 2 Kings 4:13

What she was saying was "Man of God I am very well connected, I don't think I need anything even if I need it I know where to go, so don't worry about me, I am just fine"

After she had left the room, Elisha turned to Gehazi his servant and said "What then is to be done for her" and Gehazi answered, "Verily she hath no child and her husband is old" (2 Kings 4: 14)

You can see that what Gehazi stated was an impossible situation which means this great woman's destiny is finalized. Afterall, her husband is old and perhaps would not be able to make a child. If things were left without divine intervention, this woman would die without a child; she would have forever been remembered as the great but barren Shunammite woman. Her life would have been a reflection of failure and defeat. But when Elisha heard what Gehazi said, he was more provoked and challenged to bring a change, to enforce productivity in the place of barrenness.

Elisha instructed Gehazi to bring the woman back and she came and stood in the door. And Elisha said to her; "About this season, according to the time of life, thou shalt embrace a son." (2 Kings 4:15-16)

The next verse shows the effect of the words spoken;

> *"And the woman conceived, and bare a son at the season that Elisha said unto her, according to the time of life"*
> *2 Kings 4:17*

The same woman with the same man described as old, got pregnant of a son without the help of any fertility drugs or doctors, only through the word spoken.

The word was sent forth with faith and it quickly became alive, This is what the word can do in your life as well. Hebrews 4:12 states "For the word of God is quick, and powerful, and sharper than any twoedged sword, piercing even to the dividing asunder of soul and spirit, and of joints and arrow and is a discerner of the thoughts and intents of the heart"

Note that the words of your mouth are powerful. "Thou are snared with the words of thy mouth, thou are taken with the words of thy mouth." (Proverbs 6:2). Your words can be the cop or the border control agent over your life. You can be arrested and be put in custody by it and you can be freed and acquitted by it.

In Matthew 21:18-19, the scripture states that Jesus was returning to the city in the morning and he was hungry, and he saw a fig tree along the way expecting that he would find something to satisfy his hunger. I want to think that Jesus who was over thirty years at that time was not an alien to the season of trees in his environ. He knew that the fig tree should have some fruits on it at this moment otherwise he wouldn't have had an expectation and he wouldn't have without a cause just cursed out the tree.

Just like the lives of many people, this tree was unproductive but yet occupying space. Jesus was not satisfied with the situation and he decided to cut short the existence of such tree.

You have the opportunity to use the word of God to cut short any unproductive issues of your life. You can't continue to seat in pity party, wallowing and crying thinking these emotions would bring an end to your unpleasant situation, not at all my friend. You have to take charge, you have to be violent with everything that is limiting and cutting you short. You don't have to live your life in a cycle of failure, making effort but having no result, running but in vain, working and having nothing to show for it, being married and yet live like a single individual even those who are single feels better than you who claimed to be married, raising children and they are daily acting like thugs. These situations exist to give you the opportunity to speak in faith the word of the living God over them and see the difference God can make in your life.

You always have two choices either to sit in a pity party or to act decisively to turn your situation around. Doing nothing and expecting things to change by itself is wishful thinking. Changes do not happen without a cause, they are always made to happen. They are effected through conscious effort and not wished into existence. You can act like Jesus Christ by getting mad at the unpleasant situations of your life and muster enough faith (this enough faith Jesus Christ described as big as a mustard seed) to speak a change into existence and see how your problems are solved without delay.

> *"And he left them, and went out of the city into Bethany; and he lodged there. Now in the morning as he returned into the city, he hungered. And when he saw a fig tree in the way, he came to it, and found nothing thereon, but leaves only, and said unto it, Let no fruit grow on thee henceforward forever. And presently the fig tree withered away." Matthew 21:17-19*

At the instance of Jesus' word, the tree withered away. Just as Jesus did, you will realize that those trees of sadness in your life are only there because you allowed them to remain. Those problems that have plagued your life are only in existence because you are not talking to them. Jesus was here on earth to give us examples of what we have to do to overcome. He demonstrated them that we also can have a model and pattern to emulate.

Wow! How soon the tree withers?

The effectiveness and power of words was manifested in how quickly the fig tree withered as well as in the reaction of the disciples who were amazed at the unusual incident of a tree withering just because someone commanded it to wither.

Jesus said "You can do likewise."

Many of you reading this book may be saying the days of the supernatural are gone, there are no more miracles or after all, I am not Jesus.

My friend, no one says you can ever be Jesus, but the works that Jesus did, you can do and more than He, you can bring to past.

John 14:12 says "Verily, verily I say unto you, He that believeth on me, the works that I do shall he do also; and greater works than these shall he do; because I go unto my Father."

So you don't have to be another Jesus Christ to do the impossible, all you have to be is a believer, meaning that you must have given your life to Him and He has become your Lord and Savior.

For all things are possible for those who believe in Him (Mark 9:23).

We will later see examples of people like you and I who were able to do the impossible with the words of their mouth. But you must have it in mind that in his words, he said if you only believe, you will do the works that he did and do greater works than he did.

Now going back to the story of the fig tree, Jesus did not have a second thought that the tree would dry up the moment he speaks to it. He knew the tree would obey him and the root and the trunk would rot immediately and that the branches would hence dry up and the leaves would instantly drop off.

It must be said that faith in the word is the fuel on which the word burns; the turbine which drives the miracle expected and the catalyst that quickens the action of the supernatural.

The mountain shall move!

Jesus addressed the importance of faith as to the effectiveness of the word this way;

"Verily I say unto you, If ye have faith, and doubt not, ye shall not only do this which is done to the fig tree, but. Also if ye shall say unto this mountain, Be thou removed, and be thou cast into the sea; it shall be done. And all things, whatsoever ye shall ask in prayer, believing, ye shall receive" Matthew 21: 21-22

Jesus was saying that as long as you have faith and you have no doubt in your word, you shall tell even the mountain to move and it shall respond and obey your word.

You must know that based on just these two examples of the fig tree and the mountain everything made has its hearing ability. If trees can hear the word and respond by drying up instantly and you can speak to the mountain and it would hear you and obey, therefore everything and anything would hear and obey you.

I earlier said that the problem in your life is only there because you allowed it. The crisis persists because you gave it room. The moment you decide to say enough is enough, there is no more permission for the problem to stay in your life and that the crisis should leave your life or home as you make declaration by faith, you will see the supernatural hand of God in action.

The mountains of failure and defeat, marital crisis and failing health would leave once you begin to command it to be removed.

While writing this book I have decided that some things have to be addressed in my life over my children as well as my ministry. I need to enforce some realities in my life through the word of God. I must ask my destiny to align with the Spoken Word of God. I realize that if I refuse to take charge, those things would control my life and may bring destruction and defeat so I have now decided and I am determined more than ever before to take absolute control.

Speak the Word

I have also decided that the entire congregation I am honored to lead would now on a regular basis be encouraged to make profound declarations over their lives and that of all that belong to them.

Nothing changes until they are changed. Make the decision now to effect changes in your life.

I encourage you now to put your mouth on active duty; start to move and restructure things by the power of the word in your mouth. Your tongue would be empowered the moment you have faith in what you are saying.

Chapter 4
The Impregnated Word

Chapter 4

The Impregnated Word

"So shall my WORD be that goeth forth out of my mouth: it shall not return to me void, but it shall accomplish that which I please, and it shall prosper in the thing whereto I sent it" (Isaiah 55:11)

This chapter would instruct you that the words coming out of your mouth are not just ordinary words and you shouldn't take them lightly. You must value the words you speak as God values his own word. You should have faith in them, as God has faith in his words and spoke authoritatively about his expectations of them. If you would see your words as God sees his and have the same expectation, you will be able to say with all conviction what God said in the above scripture.

About the Word

1. *It proceeds from the mouth.* With this you know that your mouth has a whole lot to do with your destiny. The words coming out of it charts the course of your being; the ultimate direction of you and your generation both born and yet unborn. God Himself said it is the words coming out of His mouth that would bring changes, not the thought of His mind, or the dreams of His head. Beloved, it has everything to do with the word.

2. *It goes forth.* Once the word is released from the mouth it has wings or legs to go forth. Words released in America can go as far as Africa even Asia. There is no distance in the spirit. Your word can go into the heaven as well as under the earth. There is no holding back and once these words are guided and empowered by faith, like in the experience of the fig tree in Matthew 21, you can expect immediate results.

3. *It can't fail.* The word spoken in faith can't fail. It can't return with disappointment or disgrace. God states that the word that proceeds from His mouth and has gone forth would not return to HIM empty. Your words should never be empty or idle and you should never allow it to cross your mind that your word in prayer would come back empty or drop on a dry ground. Your words, if spoken in faith. would not return to you void rather they would return to you bearing testimonies and good reports. You

cannot speak and see nothing happen. You cannot send your words on errand and back it with faith and not see a positive result. Speaking without faith makes your words lame and impotent; it makes the words of no effect. God has never spoken a word without result and he doesn't want you and I to have a failing expectation.

4. *It will accomplish.* God's word will never fail. It would never be defeated. It is guaranteed to accomplish whatever it is sent to do. If it was sent to heal the sick, it would do exactly that. If it was sent to cast out demons, it would accomplish that. If the word is released to drive out sadness or depression in your life, it would not fail to do that. You must have the joy of knowing that your word cannot fail and cannot be defeated. This assurance would and should keep your faith up and encourage you to speak more over your life and every situation that confronts you. I must say it here that failure and defeat is simply the failure to speak and allowing the devil to keep our mouth from making necessary declarations. The knowledge of what your word can accomplish should motivate you to make all the necessary declaration that would change your life.

5. *It will prosper in all things.* Words spoken in faith are loaded to prosper. Such utterances are pregnant with miracles and in search of a place to deliver and birth great signs and wonders. The word spoken in faith is ready to birth healing and deliverance. God states

that his words that proceeded out of his mouth will prosper in all things. As a child of God, you have the DNA of your father, you can do what your father has done and expect the same result as Him. You can see your word prosper in all things, not in just some things but in all things. With the words, you can experience an all-round success and prosperity. You can succeed on the right, left, in front and behind. You can see prosperity in all that you do. I said the word is pregnant because it is loaded and it carries all you need. The word can be used for all things and at all time without failing.

The joy I have is that the scriptures say:

"Whosoever believeth that Jesus is Christ is born of God: and every one that loveth him also this is begotten of him, For whatsoever is born of God overcometh the world: and this is the victory that overcometh the world, even our faith" 1 John 5:1, 4

Earlier I said you are a child of God and you have His DNA, and that if you act like Him, speak like Him, and have expectation just like Him, you will have what you say. The scripture above states that if you believe in Jesus and love Him, you will overcome every battles of life, there will be no defeat for you.

The following you must do:

- Don't see the problem as insurmountable, it ends the moment you stop it.

Speak the Word

- There are words in your mouth for every situation of your life.

- Think about the appropriate word for your situation based on your understanding of the Scriptures.

- Now release the word from your mind, verbalize it. Don't stop at thinking about it, release the mute button and let the word into the atmosphere.

- Wrap it up in faith.

- Send it forth with expectation.

- Prepare to celebrate its prosperity.

Chapter 5
The Commanded Word

Chapter 5
The Commanded Word

"Elias was a man subject to like passions as we are, and he prayed earnestly that it would not rain: and it rained not on the earth by the space of three years and six months. And he prayed again, and heaven gave rain, and brought forth her fruits" James 5:17-18

This scripture is a reference to Elijah's command in the days of Ahab the King of Israel when he allowed Jezebel to take his heart away from Jehovah to follow after Baal, the idol of her father. Elijah was jealous for God and in his anger decided that since Baal was considered the god of great harvest, his suspending rain and dews would prove that Baal has no power to produce a grain of corn except that God sends rain upon the earth.

The following is the direct quote of Elijah's commanded word over the land.

> *"And Elijah the Tishbite, of the inhabitants of Gilead, said unto Ahab, As the Lord God of Israel liveth, before whom I stand, there shall not be dew nor rain these years, but according to my word"* (1Kings 17:1)

Elijah knew how the principle of the commanded word works. He realized that all he needed to do was to make a faith declaration. He didn't even consult God before he spoke, he didn't call the council of prophets or call his student prophets into a time of fasting and vigorous prayer. It is not that those protocols are bad or unnecessary. I am sure Elijah, had done all these and was able to understand that praying and fasting without the ability to command situations through the word would amount to a waste of a God-given time.

He knew his God and knew that once he stood upright before Him, acted in faith and spoke the word into the atmosphere, heaven will respond accordingly.

You know that those who know their God shall be strong and do exploit (Daniel 11:32). Elijah knew his God therefore he didn't have to flinch or be scared of the apostate Ahab and his wicked devil-possessed wife, Jezebel. He went ahead and utilized the authority granted him as a child of God by speaking to the rain not to fall for what Apostle James described as a period of three years and six months.

The moment Elijah released the word into the

atmosphere, the doors of heaven were opened to let them in and God immediately responded and shut the windows of heaven that for 42 months no drop of water fell from heaven. Elijah didn't have to do a thing other than speaking.

The amazing thing in the scripture was that Elijah did not say according to the word of God, he said there shall be no rain or dew according to my word. In other words, Elijah was the one who suspended rain and dew for 42 months by his word.

James 5:17-18 notes that the same Elijah was a man like anyone of us. He wasn't a king or deity. He walked and lived among human beings yet he understood the power of commanded words by taking on rain and dew.

It was also the power of commanded words that God used to put His blessing on men due to their fellowship in unity.

> *"As the dew of Hermon, and as the dew that descended upon the mountain Zion: for there the Lord commanded the blessing, even life for evermore" (Psalms 133:3)*

You see that God commanded, in other words pronounced, His blessing over man. He used his mouth to speak the commanded word of blessing. You also can do the same.

What is a Command?

A command is an authoritative order; it is a very specific instruction to perform some action.

> *"When men are cast down, then thou shalt say, There is lifting up; and he shall save the humble person"* Job 22:29

When you are speaking the word of God upon your life you are giving authoritative order, you are giving the word specific instruction to perform some actions.

What happens in your life is a result of the order you give the word. Pay great attention to the word "authoritative". It means your word will obey you and do what you ask for. The words are prepared to perform some action.

The questions I have for you are; what order are you giving your word right now? What specific instruction are you providing? What actions do you expect to see take place?

I remember life in Africa as a very little boy in the days when there were not many vehicles to take you from one village to another. I lived the first six years of my life in a village where you have to walk about two miles before you can see a vehicle. I was old enough to walk this distance but occasionally I wanted my mom to carry me the distance. Here was a woman who had my younger sibling tied to her back because he was too young to walk the distance and she would have a heavy luggage on her head. I would start crying to be carried but the poor woman, though she would have love to heed my request wasn't in the position to do so. She would tell me "Simeon, now let us go" but I would stand at the same point and continue to cry. After some persuasion she would leave me and move on, on the two miles or so trip. After I have waited for her to come back for me with no sign of her return, the only option I had was to command my legs, "if you want to go on this journey you have to run now". At that time I would run and catch up with my mom and then walk the two miles in each other's company. I learnt very early that I had the choice of staying at the same location crying or to make the use of my legs and make progress.

This is how the word is if you have it in your mind or even in your memory and you never apply it. You will be at the same location for a long time crying without making progress.

You see that my mom did her best to motivate me to walk with her. She even waited a little bit to see if I would wise up and enjoy her company as we walk together on the way but when she realized I was unreasonable, she left me. It then became a task of running to catch up with her. Many times in my bid to catch up with her I had to run and I'd be exhausted by the time I meet up with her. Sometimes, I fell and bruised myself.

God might have encouraged you through many means in the past. You might have read books written by those before me, you might have heard messages or songs encouraging and motivating you to make a change in life but your lack of adequate actions could be responsible for your persistent struggles and perpetual crisis situation. You might have been waiting for God to speak on your behalf, or to carry you as I was doing my mom.

Let me tell you my friend, God has given you all that you need to make progress in life. If I might say it this way, you have been given the feet of faith start walking or running as the case may be. You have the ears of faith now hear what the Spirit of God is telling you. You have the eyes of faith, start seeing things as God sees them. You have the heart and mind of faith, start to think as God thinks. You have the mouth of faith, I ask that you begin to speak as God does and you will see what you expect.

You are the first prophet over your life. No pastor or prophet has the power that you have and the authority you have over your own life. I have always told people who have seen how mighty God has been in our ministry and work and wanting me to become their prayer consultant that I wasn't given such an assignment but to teach them to take charge of their own lives and destinies by the words of their own mouth. So, I must tell you here beloved, your destiny is in your hands and God will only respond to what you say.

Remember the fig tree responded to Jesus's commanded words. The rain and the dew responded to Elijah's word. None of these examples required the involvement of a third party. They did it all by themselves believing that God would honor their words. They did all they did as a mortal human beings not as angels. If they were able to do what they did as men, you also can do similarly.

Thanks to God, Jesus has said if you believe in him, the works that he did you will do and greater work you shall do. With that in mind there is nothing you cannot do.

Chapter 6

The Word of the King

Chapter 6
The Word of the King

"But ye are a chosen generation, a royal priesthood, an holy nation, a peculiar people; that ye should shew forth the praises of him who hath called you out of darkness into his marvelous light" 1 Peter 2:9

The Bible describes every believer as a member of a chosen generation, the generation that cannot be denied or forsaken. You must accept and acknowledge the reality that you are a special breed, loved by God and you truly matter to Him. To be a chosen generation means you are picked, elected and selected above and beyond others. It is done by grace not because any goodness or personal qualification and once chosen you cannot be opposed. The devil and his cohort may mount loads of accusations against you but they shall be defeated and humiliated! Who is it that can lay up accusations against God's elects? NONE!

You need to know that your words are not ordinary, worthless or unrecognizable. As an elect in Christ, you have the mandate to speak and once you speak it becomes an order with specific actions in mind.

You are also called a royal priest. As royalty, you have an unchallengeable authority; you become absolute in your words and deeds. The words of a monarch is final; no one questions him or asks him what he has done.

> *Where the word of a king is, there is power: and who may say unto him, what doest thou?" Ecclesiastes 8:4*

You don't see anyone challenging the Queen of England on any of her statements, actions or deeds. It appears that she is beyond the law of the land. The same is right for kings in Africa who are at liberty to do as they please in their kingdom. They can both kill and spare to live. That is why they call them paramount rulers. Likewise you are in the kingdom of God. You are a paramount ruler, your words are paramount, and when you speak everyone that has ears must listen, obey you and carry out all of your instructions.

To further establish your royal authority, the scripture above tells us that the word of the king carries authority and when we talk about authority, you don't have to be physically present to enforce your word, your word would be respected everywhere it is heard. It is just like a bill passed in the congress and the senate signed into law by the president. Neither the congress, the senate nor the president need to go round to see the law enforced, not at all. It would be enforced by everyone even by those who may be opposed to such law. Disobeying such carries with it certain consequences. So is your word. You can be in Texas, United States and your word being enforced in the remotest part of Africa, Asia or Central America. Remember that once you decree a thing here on earth it shall be established (Job 22:28).

If you are called a king, then start behaving like one. Stop chasing your words around, let your word go with the authority of your office and wait to see it performed. Stop negotiating with forces of disobedience rather bring them into captivity through Jesus Christ.

Chapter 7

The Word of Deliverance

Chapter 7

The Word of Deliverance

We found out in the Bible that Jesus at many times used the word to set people free from demonic attacks, especially those who were oppressed and possessed by demons. When they encountered Jesus, their lives radically changed and the operation of the devil in their lives came to an end.

> *"And they came over unto the other side of the sea, into the country of the Gadarenes. And when he was come out of the ship, immediately there met him out of the tombs a man with an unclean spirit, Who had his dwelling among the tombs; and no man could bind him, no not with chains: Because that had been often bound with fetters and chains, and the chains had been plucked asunder by him, and the fetters broken in pieces: neither could any man tame him. And always, night and day, he was in the*

mountains, and in the tombs, crying, and cutting himself with stones. But when he saw Jesus afar off, he ran and worshipped him, And cried with a lound voice, and said, What have I do with thee, Jesus thou Son of the most high God? I adjure thee by God, that thou torment me not. For he said unto him, Come out of the man, thou unclean spirit. And he asked him, What is thy name? And he answered, saying, My name is Legion: for we are many. And he besought him much that he would not send them away out of the country. Now there was there nigh unto the mountain a great herd of swine feeding. And all the devils besought him, saying, Send us into the swine, that we may enter into them. And forthwith Jesus gave them leave. And the unclean went out, and entered into the swine: and the herd ran violently down a steep placeinto the sea, (they were about two thousands;) and were choked in the sea." Mark 5:1-13

Here, we are told of how Jesus was confronted by a man with a huge (Legion) number of demons. He was described as a violent man. He had constituted himself a nuisance in the community, terrorizing people. He did not live in a civilized community as the situation of his life has excommunicated him from the community of people. Only God knows what this man was before this condition came on him. He might have been a successful attorney, accountant, medical doctor or a businessman. He might have been a family man with a wife and kids. Many would have seen his level of success and wished to be like him, but one day all these changed as the devil got hold of his life and turned him into a monster.

I strongly believe that family and friends would have tried all in their power to get him help but all to no avail. However, one day walked away and found his dwelling among the dead in the tomb. The Bible said in verse 3 and 4 that no one could bind him for they have tried with fetters and chains and he had plucked them asunder.

All these changed the moment he met Jesus. The tormentor became tormented and the terrorist submitted to higher power. Jesus didn't have to use the same method others have been applying to subdue this man, for the weapons of our warfare are not canal. He simply applied the power in his word, by saying to the demons; "Come out of the man, thou unclean spirit"

You can see that Jesus by his word subdued the demons in this man and forced them out of him and brought about his deliverance and sanity.

Equally, Jesus worked the same miracle in the life of a young boy as was recorded in Mark 9:17-26. Here was a father who brought his demon possessed son to Jesus' disciples to free him from the demon which had thrown this boy into fire and into water in an attempt to destroy him, but the disciple couldn't do anything to help this man, and when he saw Jesus he came to him asking for help. After Jesus had observed the violent nature of this demon, he opened his mouth and said; "Thou dumb and deaf spirit, I charge thee, come out of him, and enter no more into him" (v.25)

The next verse tells us that the evil spirit that has tormented this young man for a long time submitted immediately to the command of Jesus, came out of the boy and to never return again.

"And the spirit cried, and rent him sore, and came out of him: and he was as one dead; insomuch that many said, He is dead. But Jesus took him by the hand, and lifted him up; and he arose." v. 26-27

By His words, Jesus brought discomfort to the spirit of torment in the life of the young man. You also can bring torment to everyone and everything tormenting you if you will charge them to leave and never to return.

Chapter 8
Speak to the Wind

Chapter 5

Speak to the Wind

Chapter 8
Speak to the Wind

"And when they had sent away the multitude, they took him even as he was in the ship. And there were also with him other little ships. And there arose a great storm of wind, and the waves beat into the ship, so that it was now full. And he was in the hinder part of the ship asleep on a pillow: and they awake him, and say unto him. Master, carest thou not that we perish? And he arose, and rebuked the wind, an said unto the sea, Peace, be still. And the wind ceased, and there was a great clam. And he said unto them, Why are you so fearful? How is it that you have no faith? And they feared exceedingly, as said one to another, What manner of man is this, that even the wind and the sea obey him?" Mark 4:36-41

Life presents different kinds of winds. We have natural winds like hurricanes, tornadoes and typhoons. What we can do to escape these is to run from their paths and look for shelters. It has never been said that a prophet, a guru or any spiritual person besides Jesus had spoken to calm winds of any size or magnitude.

Jesus was in the boat with his twelve disciples, presumably tired after a long day of ministerial work and as they were sailing to their next destination a terrible wind emerged on the sea and his disciples were all scared and terrified. They couldn't do a thing about it until they went to Jesus accusing him of carefree attitude toward their predicament forgetting that he also was on board. They said unto him, "Master, carest thou not that we perish?" They were accusing him of negligence. But when he woke from his sleep, Jesus only had to calm the troubling of the sea with his word.

> *"And he arose, and rebuked the wind, and said unto the sea, Peace, be still. And the wind ceased, and there was a great calm." Mark 4:39*

You can see here again the tremendous power of the word. Jesus commanded even the wind and the sea and they obeyed him. The result was a great calm.

A wind may represent by a twist or turn in the course of one's life journey that makes you toil unproductively. They may be events of life determined to change the course of your life and twist you out of existence or stability. It could also be a force in opposition to your progress; as Jesus and his disciples in Mark 4:35 were on a mission to "pass over unto the other side." Jesus was to go to the other side to fulfill his mission, and along the way came this wind that was to hinder or stop him.

That is how life can be for many. In my opinion, it was the devil that moved the sea against Jesus' voyage. The wind over the sea had caused fear and panic for the disciples as you could hear grown men crying and see them shaking for the fear that they might lose their lives.

Are you faced with the contrary wind of life as you are making plans to move to the next level? Are you being threatened by the devil of doubt or fear? Are there voices of opposition and discouragement bombarding you on a daily basis telling you your vision is not possible? All these may be the wind against your voyage to progress. You see like the disciples, you may get scared and begin to buy into what you see or hear, but that is not the winning way. The winning way is Jesus' way. Stand up and confront those winds and do not relent until you see it dissipate or totally destroyed. Nothing but total calm is good for you.

The attempt of the wind on the sea was to cause team Jesus' destruction and if it couldn't destroy them, it wanted to stop them or cause them to divert from their course.

These are also the plans of every wind against your life, relationship, marriage or business to destroy, hinder or divert you from your original course. You must refuse whatever is thrown at you; you must calm the storm with the word of power in your mouth.

Just as Jesus wouldn't allow the storm on the sea to

stop him from reaching his goal you also must not be discouraged by your own "Storm on the Sea". It is just one of the many things that the devil will throw your way.

The Bible calls the devil a thief that comes to steal, to kill and to destroy. His only agenda is to bring frustration to you and to stop or slow down your wheel of progress.

"The thief cometh not, but for to steal, and to kill, and to destroy..." (John 10:10)

Whatever you are called to do and be in life, you must always remember that the devil that Peter described as your adversary is like a roaring lion, walking about, seeking whom he may devour (1Peter 5:8).

You must not allow him to catch you unaware; you must not allow his jaws to be close to you. Rather release the sword of the spirit; the word of God against him.

You are to resist him steadfast in the faith (1Peter 5:9).

Chapter 9
Speak to Death

Chapter 9

Speak to Death

Death is the end of life of a person or an organism. We however see in scriptures how what was called an end became a new beginning by the power of the word. We all know that once a thing is dead all hope on it is lost and decay sets in. On the other hand, when you use the word of God over that situation in faith, you will see a new life beginning in that situation.

So do not contemplate on giving up because someone told you anything different.

It should be stated that just about anything can die. A marriage has life, so does a business, a vision, a dream, a project and an ambition. A womb can also be dead, when this happens that state is described as barrenness. A man can also be barren especially when he has issues like low sperm count resulting in inability to impregnate a woman no matter how fertile she may be. There are different situations that could result in death but the word of God spoken by faith can bring reversal to all of them.

When a once sweet and fun filled marriage or relationship starts becoming sour and unpleasant, such is nearing death. Jesus said instead of death, he came to give us life in abundance

There are many instances in the Bible where the power of the word was exercised over death:

> *"And it came to pass the day after, that he went into a city, behold, there was a dead man carried out, the only son of his mother, and she was a widow: and much people of the city was with her. And when the Lord saw her, he had compassion on her, and said unto her, Weep not. And he came and touched the bier: and they that bare him stood still. And he said, Young man, I say unto thee, Arise. And he that was dead sat up, and began to speak. And he delivered him to his mother." Luke. 7:11-15*

The situation here was as in any that involves death, portrays hopelessness. Here is a well-known woman, probably a community woman, whose husband had died and was left with only one source of comfort, her son. The account of the Bible was that, this one son, like his father, died leaving this woman and her community in a state of utter sadness, mourning and sorrow.

The Bible notes that the woman was going in the company of many people from the city, sympathizing with her as she was going to bury her son, her only hope, her future and her source of joy. The whole community had lost hope in this young man, since the office of the medical examiner had given the final verdict that this man couldn't and wouldn't come back to life. But when a man has the word of God in his mouth, nothing is impossible. Such a man has the power to reverse terrible situations. He, like God, would call things that were not as if they were. He would see death and grave and call it life and health; this was what Jesus did in the life of this young man.

With confidence Jesus instructed those carrying the casket of this man to stop and lower it. He then moved close to this hopeless situation and with clear faith he spoke to the soul and spirit of this dead. He said 'Young man I say unto thee, Arise..." The Bible records that the dead man got up from death and he came back to life. It took just the spoken word to turn this hopeless situation around. It was the spoken word that saved the young man from decay and corruption, from that moment he started experiencing a new life.

You can do the same as Jesus; you can use the words of your mouth to bring life into your situation. You can turn around the tide over your marriage. You can speak life into your dying business instead of speaking the world's language of doubt and hopelessness. In this Christian faith, we refer to death as "sleep" because we recognize the temporality of all situations. The weak in this Christian faith will confess that he/she is strong, the poor will boldly declare in faith that he/she is rich.

Death is only final when the spoken word is not in operation. I encourage you to start speaking life into your any dead around you.

Another example is that of Lazarus of Bethany who was dead for four days. He was in fact already buried by the time Jesus got to him. His sisters had given up and told Jesus not to worry for they knew their brother's body would have been decomposing at the time. They wanted Jesus to give up on him and not to bother himself. They wanted him to just join them in weeping and mourning, but Jesus immediately sprang into action by going to the grave where Lazarus was buried and said; 'Lazarus come forth". The Bible records that without hesitation, he who was dead came back to life.

Similarly, Jesus when he overhead of the announcement of the death of Jairus' daughter in the book of Mark, looked at Jairus and said to him, "Be not afraid, only believe." Mark 5:36. One would expect that he would start consoling Jairus, but no, he only told him to be of courage and have faith. We read that when Jesus followed Jairus home he found the place in tumult as people gathered weeping and wailing greatly. (Mark 5:38)

His response to the commotion was; "Why make ye this ado, and weep? The damsel is not dead, but sleepeth" Mark 5:39

Beloved, to the average human, this was not a reasonable thing to say in situations like this, but you must understand that what makes sense to man may not be in line with the word of God. Earlier I stated that in Christian faith death is called *sleep,* poverty is called riches, and sickness is called health, for we do not speak the language of the world. We do not see things the way they appeared but the way they ought to be. We do not borrow the language of the world, rather we use the word of God to change the world.

You can see the reaction of the mourners at the statement of Jesus;

"And they laughed him to scorn…" Mark 5: 40

When you get yourself into speaking the language of faith and making prophetic declaration over your life, when suddenly you start calling things that were not as if they are, you will see people laughing at you to scorn and saying some ugly things about your faith. Some would ask why you think you are so special that whatever you say would come to pass. Know that if they did the same to Jesus, they would do it to you. The things of the Lord are obviously foolish to those of the world. And this is because we have two different cultures here, the God's culture that speaks in faith and the world culture that always wants to reason things out.

Jesus did not allow the reaction of the people affect him as he walked away from them and pursued the mission he came into that house to do. He put out all the naysayers, the doubters and took with him the father and mother of the young girl, as well as Peter, James and John. After they had entered the room where the girl was lying, he took the dead girl by hand and spoke to her. If Jesus had any belief that the girl was really dead as medical science had confirmed, he wouldn't have spoken to her. He would have spoken to her parents but rather he spoke to the girl saying; "Talitha cumi" which means "Damsel or young girl I say unto thee arise." (Mark 5:41)

Death submits to the word of faith and when Jesus had said this, the girl rose immediately.

> *'And straightway the damsel arose, and walked; for she was of the age of twelve years. And they were astonished with great astonishment." Mark 5:42*

You see that as soon as Jesus spoke into this girl's being, life came into her lifeless body and her organs resumed their functions. This is what I expect to see happen in your life, business and all that belongs to you if you will do as Jesus did.

- Speak the word of faith and hope regardless of who is near.
- Keep doubters and naysayers far away from you; they will hinder you.
- Do not allow the scornful laughter of naysayer keep you away from speaking in faith.
- Make authoritative declarations.
- Be ready to see new life and fresh blessings.
- The naysayers would eventually be astonished at what the Lord will do in your life.

DO EXACTLY WHAT JESUS DID!

Chapter 10

Speak Healing

Chapter 10

Speak Healing

"Is any among you afflicted? Let him pray... Is any sick among you? Let him call for elders of the church; and let them pray over him, anointing him with oil in the name of the Lord: And the prayer of faith shall save the sick, and the Lord shall raise him up; and if he have committed sins, they shall be forgiven him." James 5: 13-15

The Bible gave the prescription for healing; it puts it as opening your mouth to speak on it. "Is any afflicted? Let him pray."

What is praying? Jesus in Matthew 7:7 puts it as asking and he assured us that if we ask, we shall receive. And we ask by opening our mouths and making a petition. If you or anyone is sick, the way to handle it is to start speaking healing into the sick person's being. You cannot go around seeking pity or sympathy, you need neither. You are in control of your health.

In 1978, my mom was very sick and the sickness defiled medical science. Her case was like that of the woman in Mark 5, the difference was that she wasn't hemorrhaging, but something was wrong with her. She was emaciating and all tests conducted showed nothing but she was dying daily. We were all scared to see her in such condition but one thing she didn't do was to confess "I am dying." She always confessed health and wholeness, even when doctors told us she may not make it. She always said "I shall not die but live to declare the works of the Lord" and suddenly the illness that defiled medicine began to respond to the word of God.

You can acquire health using the word of God and this word is near you even in your mouth.

James in his writing states that if anyone is afflicted, let him pray. Remember he didn't say wait for others to pray for you. Of course there is nothing wrong with people praying for you, but you have to start the process, having faith in whatsoever you say and have no doubt, you will have what you have asked.

Jesus said that no matter how much you have prayed, no matter how much you have placed demands and no matter how much you have petitioned, it is just not enough. There is more in God and your needs can never exhaust the resources and supply found in him.

"Hitherto have ye asked nothing in my name: ask, and ye shall receive, that your joy may be full." John 16:24

Jesus encourages you to take advantage of what is yours

and freely given and that by asking whatever it is that you need, which in this case it may be healing on any part of your body, over your children, spouse or others, you will receive what you ask.

It has always been said that there is no distance in prayer. You can stand in proxy for anyone and at any place and you should expect that God will answer and they shall receive the miracle you petitioned on their behalf.

I remember one of our deaconesses whose sister-in-law in Nigeria was barren for many years. During one Sunday service, something unusual happened as God moved me by the Holy Spirit to once again pray for those who have been waiting on God for children. I said "once again" because God has given us grace to pray over those without children and with abiding testimonies of pregnancies resulting in children. During this meeting, this woman came to the altar on behalf of her sister-in-law and her brother who have been married for a long time without a child. I prayed as I was led by God for her and many others who were there asking that the Spirit of God would take over their womb and whatever has been hindering their ability to produce children be neutralized. She believed the prayer and her sister–in-law in Nigeria received a supernatural touch the same time we prayed. Like all that stood at the altar that day, she became pregnant that month, gave birth to a baby, and has henceforth had other children.

See, the prayer was made at 6706 West Airport Blvd. Houston Texas and God moved upon someone in

Lagos, Nigeria. So, I submit to you, there is no distance in prayer.

You should call to mind what the word of Isaiah 55: 11 says;

> *"The word that goeth out of your mouth will not return void, it will accomplish that which you are pleased and prosper in that which you have sent it."*

So you don't have to worry about the distance, all you have to do is to release the word.

You can send the word of healing to someone who may be sick lying in a hospital bed even though they are at the other end of the earth. If you have faith you will hear the good news of their healing.

Remember God is omnipresent, he is available everywhere at the same time and his power is not limited by distance. Of course in these days of world wide web when the world has become a global village, if you can send an e-mail or a text message from one end of the earth to another and can be received in seconds you can equally send the word of God from one end of the earth and it shall be effective at the other end. Knowing this, you can be in Beijing, China and speak unto the life of someone in Zanzibar land and heaven will act on it as long as you pray in faith.

I remember the case of a woman who met me in a meeting in Columbus, Ohio. Her father in Nigeria was sick of prostate cancer and has been in the hospital for a while because his case was getting worse by the day. During my ministration, I gave a testimony of a lady who was delivered and healed by the power of God from stage 3 cancer and that God is still in the business of healing all manners of sicknesses and illnesses. Her faith leaped and when I called out those who are sick or those with sick family members whether they were in Columbus or elsewhere, she came out and whispered in my ears that her father has been lying in the hospital in Lagos Nigeria with a case of cancer. I prayed with her as well as others. A few weeks later, this woman's pastor who was my host in that meeting called to testify that the woman's dad was discharged from the hospital as his cancer was getting into remission.

Let not the distance between you and anyone you are praying for be a discouragement. As you pray, the wind and wings of the Holy Spirit will take the prayer prayed in faith to anyone you have in mind.

Jesus went further by saying something very profound, "You have to pray for yourself not me praying for you."

> *"At that day ye shall ask in my name: and I say not unto you, that I will pray the Father for you:" John 16: 26*

Here you see that prayer from your lips to the ears of God makes a great difference. Jesus was encouraging you to pray for yourself. He said, I am not telling you to sit down watching or looking, thinking that I have to do all things for you, no! You have to go to God, the Father by yourself.

This also discourages you from going from one prayer house to the other seeking for prayers. You are the prayer house. You are the best prophet for yourself. Your prayer works more effectively over your life more than anyone else's can do for you. God is waiting for you to petition him.

Why would God answer you as he did Jesus?

> *"For the Father himself loveth you, because ye have loved me, and have believed that I came out from God" John 16:27*

The reason why God answered Jesus at all times and he never prayed a prayer never answered was that God loved him. And the same Jesus said in the above scripture that God loves you and if so, all your prayers shall be answered. And if you have that assurance that your prayer shall be answered, then go ahead and pray with a godly expectation.

> *"Is any afflicted? Let him pray…" James 5:13*

God heals the smallest of sickness as well as the biggest of it, and he would not leave the moderate one behind. The Bible has a record of healing of paralysis, blood related sickness, as well as insanity. While you may be going from place to place looking for a specialist, God is the general physician; he knows how to deal with the intricacies of your life.

> *"The great physician is here, Jesus the compassionate. His word brings healing, his word brings wholeness"*

These are the words of a song we used to sing when

I was very young growing up in my Dad's church and sincerely, I believe the word today as I did then. My faith in the word set me free from yearly sickness in 1984. It happened that I used to fall sick every October and the diagnosis was always inconclusive but one day my Dad said; "Simeon, I am tired of this your yearly sickness, whatever is behind it must cease its operation today". I saw that he was pretty mad with this pain and weakness. He got a bucket of water after he had read some scriptures, he prayed over the water and said, "go take a bath and once you come out of the shower, the sickness would be gone and never to come back again."

I was encouraged to sing the song quoted above and I did as I was instructed. I came out of that shower lighter than I was before heading there and to the glory of God I can testify that since October 1984, I have never had a repeat of that sickness again.

You can see that my Dad didn't do a thing other than speaking the word of God and I only followed after the instruction and believed that the end will come to my then sickness and God honored both the prayer and my faith.

I like the way the Bible puts the responsibility and the burden of making a change on us.

> "And these signs shall follow them that believed; In my name shall they cast out devils; they shall speak with new tongues; They shall take up serpents; and if they drink any deadly thing, it shall not hurt them; they shall lay hands on the sick, and they shall recover." Mark 16:17-18

Chapter 11
Speak Abundance

Chapter 11
Speak Abundance

Many people today are trapped in the vicious circle of lack, penury and begging and some for generations. Some of these people are in the households of faith yet they are not maximizing their covenant privileges in Christ. Some have been taught wrongly that poverty is synonymous with holiness. The Bible never taught us that poverty is a sign or evidence of purity or holiness quite on the contrary; the pleasure of God is that you live in prosperity.

> *"Beloved, I wish above all things that thou mayest prosper and be in health even as your soul prospereth." 3 John 2*

This prayer represents the heart of God for you and I. We are to live our lives in plenty, not in lack, not as beggars or depending on the state to feed them and their family.

We as God's children should determine the state of the world's economy, not the other way round. Our father owns it all and we have the right as children to own it all as well.

> *"The silver is mine, and the gold is mine, saith the Lord of hosts." Haggai 2:8*

Jesus realized the need for money when he was approached by the tribute (tax) collectors and was expected to pay taxes for himself and Peter. At this time Judas Iscariot, the ministry's treasurer, was nowhere to be found and without this payment Jesus would have been embarrassed. What did he do?

He sent Peter to the sea with his hook to fish with the instruction: "the first fish you catch will bring you money needed for the tributes." Peter did as instructed and came back with money enough to pay the tributes or taxes of both of them.

> *"And when they were come to Capernaum, they that received tribute money came to Peter, and said, Doth not your master pay tribute? He saith, Yes. And when he come into the house, Jesus prevented him, saying, What thinkest thou, Simon? Of whom do the kings of the earth take custom or tribute? Of their own children, or of strangers? Peter saith unto him, Of strangers. Jesus saith unto him, Then are the children of the free. Notwithstanding, lest we should offend them, go thou to the sea, and cast an hook, and take up the fish that first cometh up; and when thou hast opened his mouth, thou*

> *shalt find a piece of money: take that, and give unto them for me and thee." Matthew 17:24-27*

If you do not have money, you will offend many people. You will offend your landlord, the bank that financed your car or home, your children who look up to you for sustenance, your wife and family whom you would not be able to stand with financially.

It has always been said that a poor man speaking is not better than a barking dog.

> *"A feast is made for laughter, and wine maketh merry: but money answereth all things." Ecclesiastes 10: 19*

Let no man deceive you that it is wrong to pray to God to bless you monetarily, as it is the will of God to prosper you and to make all grace abound toward you that you will have all things in sufficiency. It is a known fact that a poor, no matter how old he is will be a servant to the rich, no matter how young he may be.

The word of God told us that as long as you obey God, he would pour his blessing upon you.

> *"And it shall come to pass, if thou shalt hearken diligently unto the voice of the Lord thy God, to observe and to do all his commandments which I command thee this day, that the Lord thy God will set thee on high above all nations of the earth: And all these blessing shall come on thee, and overtake thee, if thou shalt hearken unto the voice of the Lord thy God Blessed shalt thou be in the city, and blessed shalt thou be in the field. Blessed shall be*

the fruit of thy body, and the fruit of thy ground, and the fruit of thy cattle, the increase of thy kine, and the flock of thy sheep. Blessed shall be thy basket and thy store. Blessed shalt thou be when thou comest in, and blessed shalt thou be when thou goest out. The Lord shall cause thine enemies that rise up against thee to be smitten before thy face: they shall come out against thee one way, and flee before thee seven ways. The Lord shall command the blessing upon thee in thy storehouses, and in all that thou settest hand unto; and he shall bless thee in the land which the Lord thy God giveth thee. The Lord shall establish thee a holy people unto himself, as he hath sworn unto thee, if thou shalt keep the commandments of the Lord thy God, and walk in his ways. And all the people of the earth shall see that thou art called by the name of the Lord; and they shall be afraid of thee. And the Lord shall make thee plenteous in goods, in the fruit of thy body, and in the fruits of thy cattle, and the fruit of thy ground, in the land which the Lord sware unto thy fathers to give thee. The Lord shall open unto thee his good treasure, heaven to give the rain unto thy land in his season, and to bless all the work of thine hand: and thou shalt lend to nations, and thou shall not borrow. And the Lord shall make thee the head and not the tail; and thou shall be above only, and thou shall not be beneath; if thou hearken unto the commandments of the Lord thy God, which I command thee this day, to observe and do them."
Deuteronomy 28: 1-13

As much as it is not my intention to make this scripture the center point of this chapter but I just can't but summarize the scripture in the light of this subject.

1. If you obey God's commandment and keep them, there is no way divine blessings can elude you.

2. God's blessing will come upon you, run after you and overtake you, this means you will have all-around blessings.

3. You will be blessed both in the city and in the field. No nation will be hostile to you. Since the blessing has overtaken you, before you arrive at any country, city or town, blessing would be there waiting for you. That was why Isaac in Genesis 26 prospered in Gerar of the Philistine even in the time of famine. Blessings will always be upon you and around you and ahead of you.

4. There shall be no barrenness in your life and in the lives of all that God has given to you including the fruit of your ground, the fruit of your cattle, the increase of your kine and of your sheep.

5. Your basket and your storehouse, in our contemporary world meaning your bank account shall be blessed.

6. You shall be blessed in your coming in and in your going out.

7. Your enemies that shall rise up against you in one way shall run from before you seven ways and the Lord shall beat them down.

8. Your storehouse (bank account) shall be blessed and so shall everything you set your hand upon to do.

9. The Lord will establish you as a holy people unto himself.

10. The whole earth will see the glory of God upon you and call you by the name of the Lord and shall have reverence for you.

11. The Lord will make you plentiful in goods also in the fruit of your body, of your cattle and fruit of your ground.

12. The Lord will open his good treasure unto you and heaven to rain unto your land in its season, the work of your hand shall be blessed and you will loan to nations and you will never borrow.

13. You shall be the head at all times and not the tail, above and not below.

When you read all these you will come to realize that God wants you to prosper as long as you obey him and follow after his words. You also see that abundance or prosperity is not limited to money but to and all things. The word is needed to change poverty into prosperity.

Jesus by his word fed nearly twenty thousand people with only five loaves and two fishes, all he did was speak upon the five leaves and two fishes and abundance resulted.

> *"And when it was evening, his disciples came to him, saying, This is a desert place, and the time is now past;*

send the multitude away, that they may go into the villages, and buy themselves victuals. But Jesus said unto them, They need not depart; give them to eat. And they say unto him, We have here but five loaves, and two fishes. He said, Bring them hither to me. And he commanded the multitude to sit down on the grass, and took the five loaves, and the two fishes, and looking up to heaven, be blessed, and brake, and gave the loaves to his disciples to the multitude. And they did all eat, and were filled: and they took up of the fragments that remained twelve baskets full." Matthew 14: 15-20

Here, we can see how Jesus used his word to bring supply to a point of lack and satisfied the longings of the people. He exercised his authority over lack and want. You can also do the same if you will have his kind of faith.

The disciples had a different kind of faith see how they responded to him when he said "They need not depart; give them to eat" v 16.

They responded by saying, "We have here but five loaves, and two fishes." v 17

What their faith was saying was, this would be grossly inadequate, but Jesus' faith was, that little can become much through the power of the word.

You also must see whatever you have in your hands now as much no matter how little it appears to be. Just open your mouth and start speaking abundance; ask the heavens to open upon you and rain upon you the abundance of God's treasure. When you do this, have expectations because you can only see what you expect. You must see God as your Jehovah Jireh, the one who met Abraham and blessed him. See him as your El-shaddai, the Lord who is able to do more than you can think or pray for.

> *"Now unto him that is able to do exceeding abundantly above all that we ask or think according to the power that worketh in us" Ephesians 3:20*

All that God has is yours as long as you are his child. Do not live your life in lack and want. You can change your situation, change it now by the power of his word in your mouth. Make sure you speak your blessings into being. If your need is a child, you can speak the child into being. If it is peace, Jesus is the prince of peace. Whatever you need, God can and he will supply.

Chapter 12

Believe and Speak

Chapter 12
Believe and Speak

"We having the same spirit of faith, according as it is written, I believed, and therefore have I spoken; we also believe, and therefore speak." 2 Corinthians 4:13

Speaking to the Corinthian church here, Apostle Paul taught them that, a believer who has the spirit of faith, would believe in both the spoken and written word of God over his/her life. Therefore with faith in God the believer would speak that which he/she has believed into existence. Without faith whatever word spoken is a waste and without speaking, the word the faith in us is equally wasted.

The same Paul stated;

"...The word is nigh thee, even in thy mouth, and in thy heart: that is, the word of faith, which we preach; That if thou shalt confess with thy mouth the Lord Jesus, and

shalt believe in thine heart that God hath raised him from the dead, thou shalt be saved. For with the heart man believeth unto righteousness and with mouth confession is made unto salvation." (Romans 10:8-10)

We now know that it is one thing to have faith, it is another to make the faith work, and we make faith work by confessing that which we have believed.

In 2 Corinthians 4:13, it was said the motivation for our speaking is because we have believed, because we have faith that whatever we say would come to pass. You will be timid and emotionally paralyzed if you never allow your faith to speak. You have to make known what you believe for your life. You have to say what your heart has believed.

… Because we believe, therefore we speak. There is an unusual boldness that normally comes with faith and with that boldness you should speak into existence what you want in your life.

The psalmist said in faith of himself;

"I shall not die, but live, and declare the works of the Lord." (Psalm 118:17)

That was the statement of a convinced man, even though he died physically, his legacy and name never died. You can claim the same for you and your loved ones.

You can take hold of the word in Isaiah 54 in faith and personalize each promise over your life as follow:

"I will sing and break forth into singing, I will enlarge the place of my tent, and stretch for the curtain of my habitation, I will extend the cords and strengthen my stakes; For I will break forth on the right hand and on the left; and my seed shall inherit the Gentiles and my desolate places shall be inhabited. I shall not be afraid for I shall not be ashamed or confounded. I shall not be put to shame and the shame of my youth shall be forgotten." (v 1-4)

You can also say the following over your life:

"For I shall go out with joy, and be led forth with peace: the mountains and the hills shall break forth before me into singing, and all the trees of the field shall clap their hands for me. Instead of thorn shall come up the fir tree, and instead of brier shall come up the myrtle tree: and it shall be to the Lord for a name, for an everlasting sign that shall not be cut off" (Isaiah 55:12-13 adapted)

Conclusion

"Now when he had ended all his sayings in the audience of the people, he entered into Capernaum. And a centurion's servant, who was dear to him, was sick, and ready to die. And when he heard of Jesus, he sent unto him elders of the Jews, beseeching him that he would come and heal his servant. And when they came to Jesus, they besought him, saying, That he was worthy for whom he should do this: For he loveth our nation, and he hath built us a synagogue. Then Jesus went with them. And when he was now not far from the house, the centurion sent friends to him, saying unto him, Lord, trouble not thyself: for I am not worthy that thou shouldest enter under my roof: Wherefore neither thought I myself worthy to come unto thee: but say in a word, and my servant shall be healed. For I also am a man set under authority, having under me soldiers, and I say unto one, Go, and he goeth; and to another, Come and he cometh; and to my servant, Do this, and he doeth it. When Jesus heard these things, he marveled at him, and turned him about, and said unto the people that followed him, I say unto you, I have not found so great faith, no, not in Israel. And they that were sent, returning to the house, found the servant whole that had been sick." Matthew 8:5-13 (GNT)

The word works. The centurion above understood the power of the word.

In these scriptures, we can clearly see the efficacy of the spoken word. The man who sought Jesus' help was not a Jew, he was a Roman and a military man. He was in fact referred to as the controller of a troop of hundred soldiers (a centurion). He was a man of influence but needed help from the Master. When Jesus approached his house he asked that Jesus did not need to come under his roof for he was not worthy of his visit. He insisted that all he needed from Jesus was a word and his servant who was sick would be made whole.

Jesus called this act a display of great faith such as he has never found before. The faith of this centurion amazed Jesus. Jesus observed that this was a stranger to the Jewish religion; he wasn't a religious man, yet he had developed so much faith in the things of God and especially in the teachings of Jesus Christ. The agent of healing in this man's servant was the spoken word of Jesus Christ which was activated by the faith of the centurion.

You know when a word is spoken by God through his servant or through the written word, it needs to be activated or else it would be dormant and of no importance. Just like your credit card would not work until you activate it, so is the word of God over your life when it is not activated. Let us see what the spoken word did in this situation. First let us see the problem:

Speak the Word

The centurion's servant was:

- Sick in bed.
- Unable to move.
- Suffering terribly.

One would think that this young man would need:

- A medical doctor to take care of his sickness.
- A physical therapist to help him with use of limbs.
- A pain management expert to help deal with his suffering.

This shows that this man's case was multi-leveled and one wouldn't think that just a word spoken from a distance would have been sufficient to bring about restoration but it did. The word:

- Raised him from his sick bed.
- Reactivated his limbs for mobility.
- Eliminated his pain.

You have seen through the pages of this book how much influence you have over your life and your current realities. While the devil would rather have you wallow in pity and languish in pain managing struggles and difficulty, Jesus is calling you to tap into the abundant life he has offered you by his death, burial and resurrection. The secret to unlocking your access to this higher level of victorious living is the word of God.

The written word spoken by you is one of your greatest

assets in reconfiguring your life and destiny for good. A closed mouth is indeed a closed destiny. Nothing moves unless you move it by your word and decrees. Invest time in your study of God's word to familiarize yourself with his settled promises over your life and begin to enforce them by your pronouncements of faith. Believe that as you speak, the Spirit of God is at work supervising the enactment of your decrees.

As a child of God, your destiny is to live a limitless life where nothing is impossible with you. Your mouth is the activating portal of this glorious destiny. Open your mouth and begin to declare the word. I look forward to hearing your testimonies.

www.ingramcontent.com/pod-product-compliance
Lightning Source LLC
LaVergne TN
LVHW051844080426
835512LV00018B/3052